Revealing Truth

Providing Convincing Answers to 'YOUR' Profound Questions

BY

Frenica Williams

INTRODUCTION

Imagine you are standing before a potential labourer (an unbeliever) of the kingdom of God. They ask a question that may determine whether they join the kingdom and become a citizen. Their decision is based on your answer to their question. How would you answer? Yes, I know only God can change a heart. However, I don't think the book of ***Matthew 9:37,*** where Jesus stated, “The harvest truly is plentiful, but the labourers are few,” was for no reason. In addition, Paul, whom God chose by His grace and converted to reveal His son in him, preached among the heathen and stated, “I take pleasure in infirmities, in reproaches, in necessities, in persecutions for Christ's sake” .... let me not get too ahead of myself, you can tell by now that he is one of my favourite Apostles in the Bible.

Let's get back to the main idea; He clearly states in **I Corinthians 3:6,** “that you can plant, I can help water but God gives the increase.” This means we all have a role to play in adding to His (God’s) kingdom, and we leave the rest to God. As simple as it may seem to answer a question relating to your faith, it's of utmost importance that you answer and know how to answer it biblically. A brother of mine (in the faith) once told me, “How you answer someone's question can cause them to give their life over to God or withdraw.” So, I ask you, “What kind of impact would you like to have on a non-believer or even a believer's life?” Don’t get me wrong, we do have some believers who are unable to answer some questions adequately. The Bible is monumental; it's endless, and the more we read, the more knowledge and wisdom we receive concerning our faith. The Psalmist declares in **Psalm 119:130,** “The entrance of thy word giveth light; it giveth understanding unto the simple.” So, we have all started simple, not knowing anything; nevertheless, the more we dive into the word, the more we are enlightened. So, let me enlighten you a bit. You do the rest by being committed to reading the word of God and with the help of the holy spirit. For now, read this book to the end and *be ready to give an answer to every man that asketh you a reason for the hope that is in you,* **1st Peter 3:15.** You’ll find some common questions that myself and others have been asked. All answers to questions are from the word of God—as scriptures references are used for brief elaboration and clarity. I encourage you to have your Bible next to you as you read this book for **2 Timothy 2:15,** which says, “Study to shew thyself approved unto God, a workman that needeth not to be ashamed, rightly dividing the word of truth.” My brothers and sisters, you are needed! Don’t stop studying, don’t stop labouring for His kingdom.

Table of Contents

QUESTION I

Is the Bible a regular book?

Have you ever purchased a new item and got excited about using it? Because it is new, you do not actually know how to use it. Luckily, the item came with a manual and instructions to guide you on how to operate it. You read the manual, and you apply it. You may get it right the first time, and probably not. Nevertheless, you got it operating and received your money's worth. Just as you need instructions on how to operate that generator, fan, phone, and even a water bed, it's the same as you would need instructions on how to operate in our new life for the Lord Jesus.

Let's look at it like this: you used your money to buy a generator, so you expect it to be in good working condition because you paid value for it. However, it does not work that way. To enjoy your money's worth, you have to power-start it and follow the instructions in the manual. In this illustration, the money is your "faith"; however, you had to activate it in order to receive your salvation and walk into your new life **(Acts 16:31).** You are in your new life; still, you do not know where to start and how to fully function in it, just as you did not know how to operate that generator.

But blessed are we that our saviour left a manual to ensure that we operate and are guided on this new journey that we have chosen to embark on. Our saviour is ensuring we are getting our faith's worth, just as any retailer would try to ensure we get our money's worth from anything we purchase. The only difference is our saviour's manual is settled with no expiration date and guarantees effective functioning if we follow it consistently and faithfully.

This manual is called the Bible. As my father, mentor, and Apostle Donald Purge would say, "Basic Instructions Before Leaving Earth," and I would call it the good news, history, our future, and endless adjectives to describe this quick and powerful, sharper than any two-edged sword manual. If you have no faith, you cannot truly apply this manual to receive newness in your life. So, let's break down the stigma about the "BIBLE."

I chose to answer this question first because all the other questions and answers rely on the BIBLE. I am answering this question to clarify that this manual is efficient and is not like any other book. Yes! We say—like any other book—the BIBLE is written by men. However, my question to you is this: has any book you read left an impact on your life, even though they were written by man? If your answer is yes, then let's dive in deeper. Just as those men who wrote regular books caused you to change your behaviour, become a better person, or become better at something. The Bible can do that and more. Yes, a regular man like you and I wrote the Bible. However, there were forty men who were inspired by God! As **2 Timothy 3:16** states, "**All scripture is given by inspiration of God, and is profitable for doctrine, for reproof, for correction, for instruction in righteousness.**"

Shedding Light On The Luminary (God)

God First Inspired Nothing Into Something

From the beginning of time, God spoke to His people. Let's rewind: prior to speaking to man, He spoke to nothing, and that nothing became something. Darkness became light (**Genesis 1:3**), and the earth, the dry land, brought forth fruitfulness **(Genesis 1: 11-**

12). God inspired this earth into its very existence just by speaking to it. I encourage you to read all of **Genesis 1 and 2 to** experience the Luminary yourself.

The First Man God Inspired

According to **Genesis2:19-20, the** first man that God inspired was Adam. God instructed Adam to perform a tasking responsibility, which was to name all the animals. **Genesis 2:19 states, "And out of the ground the Lord God formed every beast of the field, and every fowl of the air; and brought them unto Adam to see what he would call them: and whatsoever Adam called every living creature, that was the name thereof."** Adam was divinely inspired by God to name those animals, the names that we still call them to this day. To be divinely inspired speaks of a supernatural force, causing a person to experience a creative desire. You and I wonder where Adam got all those names and how to distinguish them. Scientists have estimated that there are a total of 8.7 million animal species living on earth, many of which are yet to be discovered. There is no way Adam could have executed such creativity without the mind of God embedded within him. God could have simply named them all, but He allowed us to see man's capability with His involvement. The word of God says, **"To see what he would call them,"** he allowed Adam to use his free will to speak into the atmosphere, calling each animal by name, knowing that it would be permanent because of His involvement. God initiated it all; this was not something that just happened; it was a revelation.

A revelation is something that is hidden and has been made known. Each animal had its name before they came into existence. God used Adam to bring their name from the spiritual into the natural. It flowed from the mind of God into the mind of Adam and out of his mouth into the earth. His word says, "And **whatsoever Adam called every living creature, that was the name thereof."** These are the names that we use to identify any animal in sight today.

If we don't believe in the Bible, why do we call each animal by their name? Knowing that Moses, who God inspired, wrote the book of Genesis and exposed us to what was revealed unto him by God. **Genesis 2:20 says, "And Adam gave names to all cattle, and to the fowl of the air, and to every beast of the field."** Some may not believe in the Bible but still find themselves doing what the Bible says, whether they acknowledge it or not. We are definitely doers of the word, unconsciously and consciously.

Let's Talk about my Favourite Apostle

Apostle Paul's Journey with the Luminary (GOD)

Paul, originally named Saul of Tarsus, was one of the greatest leaders in history. We know that he was a prosecutor of the church **(Acts 8)** before his encounter with God **(Acts 9)**. He wrote thirteen books of the New Testament, not by his own will but by the revelation of Jesus Christ.

In the epistle of Paul, the Apostle to the Galatians, he elaborated on his journey and how it wasn't by his might nor strength that he could deliver the gospel. Paul states in **Galatians 1:11-12, "But I certify you, brethren, that the gospel which was preached of me is not after man. For I neither received it of man, nor was I taught it, but by the revelation of Jesus Christ."** Shortly, I will go into detail concerning the fascinating aspect of this chapter. Paul could make such statements because, as mentioned at the beginning, he was a prosecutor and didn't know anything about the gospel until he encountered Jesus Christ on the road to Damascus. In verses **3** and **4 of Acts 9, it** says, "as **he journeyed, he came near to Damascus: and suddenly there shined round about him a light from heaven. And he fell to the earth, and heard a voice saying unto him, Saul, Saul why persecutest thou me?** This encounter with Jesus Christ brought forth such creativity to write the mind of God on paper and preach all around. Let's dive into the remaining verses of **Galatians** chapter **1: 17-23.**

"Neither went I up to Jerusalem to them which were apostles before me; but I went into Arabia, and returned again unto Damascus. *18* ***Then after three years, I went up to Jerusalem to see Peter, and abode with him fifteen days.*** *19* ***But other of the Apostles saw I none, save James the Lord's brother.*** *20* ***Now the things which I write unto you, behold, before God, I lie not.*** *21* ***Afterwards I came into the regions of Syria and Cilicia;*** *22* ***And was known by face to face unto the churches of Judea which were in christ:*** *23* ***But they had heard only, That he which persecuted us in times past now preacheth the faith***

which he once destroyed.** 24 **And they glorified God in me."

Paul was ensuring that the people of Galatia knew that the gospel he preached was divinely revealed to him by God and that it was not taught to him by the Apostles. These contrasts what he was taught about the law by a Pharisee named Gamaliel, a doctor of the law. In the book of Acts 22, Paul defends himself and explains to the people who he was before the auction to preach the gospel came upon him. He went into detail in verse 3 by saying, "***I am verily a man which am a Jew born of Tarsus, a city in Cilicia, yet brought up in this city at the feet of Gamaliel, and taught according to the perfect manner of the law of the fathers.***" Here, we see that Paul's persecution of the church was a reflection of what he was taught. **(Acts 22:4, "And I persecuted this way unto death, binding and delivering into prisons both men and women)** He was inspired, encouraged, motivated, and persuaded by Gamaliel that their teaching was the right one, which resulted in him defending what he believed to the fullest extent. Acts 7:58 is where Saul was first mentioned in the Bible These contrasts, and it declares, "***And cast him out of the city, and stoned him: and the witnesses laid down their clothes at a***

young man's feet, whose name was Saul." According to history, laying down clothes was a symbolic gesture that death or violence was to take place. From the above scripture, we can tell that (1) Saul didn't participate in stoning Stephen, and two (2) he was trusted by the witnesses. This leads to the conclusion that Saul approved the violence meted out to Stephen. **Acts 8:1** says, ***"And Saul was consenting unto his death. And at that time there was a great prosecution against the church which was at Jerusalem; and they were all scattered abroad throughout the regions of Judaea and Samaria, except the Apostles."***

It confirms Saul's first and continuous persecution of the followers of Christ.

Paul's past was evident to everyone, so he wrote to the churches explaining his transition from a persecutor to a gospel preacher. Paul's transformation was not a regular one; it was his encounter with Christ that made it unorthodox.

Let's explain what he meant in (**Galatians 1: 17-24).** In Paul's effort to ensure that **Galatians 1:11-12** was a fact, he explained that when he was called by the grace of God and chosen **(Acts 9:15)** to preach among the heathen, he immediately conferred not with flesh and blood but by the leading of the Holy Spirit **(Galatians 1:16).** Paul explains that after his consultation with God, he never went up to Jerusalem to meet the other Apostles, in fact; after his encounter with God, he had lost his sight and was instructed by God to go into a city, and there he would be told what to do. The first-person Paul met was Ananias, whom the Lord spoke to in a vision to meet him. As expected, Ananias was familiar with that name because he persecuted the church. However, God told Anania through revelation that "Saul was a chosen vessel." Ananias was obedient and went his way in search of brother Saul. He laid his hands on Saul, and he received his sight, was baptised, and filled with the Holy Ghost. What I love about this is that God ensured that Paul (Brother Saul) went through different stages before being used as his vessel to preach the Gospel. He was first someone who did not believe in the Gospel, the death, burial, and resurrection of Jesus Christ. He then had an encounter with God to receive transformation and immediate belief in our Lord and saviour; after which he was baptised and filled with the Holy Ghost. After all of this, Paul went straight into the synagogues, preaching that Christ is the son of God **(Acts 9:20)**. He went into Arabia and returned to Damascus, and he was also on the run because they wanted to kill him. After three years, Paul finally went to Jerusalem and met up with Peter, who he was with for just fifteen days. This proves that none of the Apostles who walked with Jesus while He was on earth had the chance to teach Apostle Paul anything concerning the gospel, but it was by the revelation of Jesus Christ **(Galatians 1:12).**

Paul had a profound encounter with The Luminary (God). He was a simple man inspired by the wrong doctrine; however, when he allowed Jesus Christ into your ?, he became an Apostle whom God inspired to write the mind of God on paper for us so that we can be next in line to have our personal encounters with God and receive the transformation Paul once had. Not only did Paul write to us, but God used forty vessels of honour to speak to His people to give us hope in Him. Romans **15:4** declares, "**For whatsoever things were written afore time were written for our learning, that we through patience and comfort of the scriptures might hope**." The words that you see in the Bible today is not of Paul, Moses, James, John, Peter, or Isaiah; it is not of men, although written by men. **2 Peter 1:21** states, **"Knowing this first, that no prophecy of the scripture is of any private interpretation. For the**

prophecy came not in old time by the will of man: but holy men of God spoke as they were moved by the Holy Ghost."

The Bible is not a regular book; the words you read from it are alive. It is God himself. **John 1:1 says, "In the beginning was the word, and the word was with God, and the word was God."**

I hope you read and pray about this. May you understand that God speaks to His people. He will never abandon us without something to direct our path. His word is that direction; **It's a lamp unto our feet, and a light unto our path,"** Psalms 119:105.

We are going somewhere, and we cannot reach without the word of God directing us on the right path. May you receive the revelation that God speaks to His people from the beginning of time; as Hebrews 1:1-2says, **"God who at sundry times and in divers manners spake in time past unto the fathers by the prophets, hath in these last days spoken unto us by his son, whom he hath appointed heir of all things, by whom also he made the worlds."** Even now, He speaks to us through His words and many other ways. Do not prevent what God will say to you today from reaching your ears and entering your heart. Pick up a

Bible, pray to your maker to reveal something to you, start reading, and position yourself to hear from God. **Matthew 11:15** says, "**He that hath ears to hear, let him hear.**"

Sometimes, we question if everything in the Bible is, in fact, true or whether someone had written something different from God's inspiration. Our job as children of God is not to uncover that but to trust that God will reveal to us what needs to be revealed by His Spirit. More importantly, we can depend on **Revelation 22:18-19, which says, "For I testify unto every man that heareth the words of the prophecy of this book, If any man shall add unto these things, God shall add unto him the plagues that are written in the book: And if any man shall take away from the words of the book of this prophecy, God shall take away his part out of the book of life, and out of the holy city, and from the things which are written in this book."**

Those who wrote the Bible, rewrote it in different versions, and those who preached the word will be reprimanded if they added anything that God didn't approve of or removed from what God has inspired them to write or preach. Therefore, our job is to receive the word as we see it and hear it. As **1 Thessalonians 2:13** states, "**For this cause also thank we God without ceasing, because, when ye received the word of God which ye heard of us, ye received it not as the word of men, but as it is truth, the word of God, which effectually worketh also in you that believe.**"

May we receive the words of the Bible as they come from God and not from men because it is not like regular books. The Bible is a Book of books. It's a compilation of sixty-six different books.

QUESTION 2

How do we know God is real?

A question commonly thrown at believers, and as one of them, the scripture that comes to my mind is

Psalms 14

"The fool hath said in his heart, There is no God."

There is an implied question from the passage above: Who is God? I think many people don't understand who God is, and that's why they do not seem to think there is a God. Therefore, let's bring clarity to the term God. To answer that question, who is God? The Lord is God. Deuteronomy 6:4 says, "***Hear, O Israel: The Lord our God is one Lord" a***nd Psalm 18: 31 says, '***For who is God save the Lord?'*** So, God is Lord, the Lord is God. We are not focusing on the "one' part; we are acknowledging that God is Lord. The term Lord signifies authority, power, ownership, sovereignty, and pre-eminence. We are all familiar with the term. According to freedictionary.com,

"Landlord" refers "to a person who owns a property and allows another person to use it for a fee." In order to show that the Land belongs to someone, ``Lord was placed after the term land, bringing the new term "landlord." Just as the term Lord needed to be used to show ownership of land, the same way Lord is used to show ownership over all things. In this case, no other term is placed before the Lord because God is not the owner of any particular thing, but He is the ruler and maker of all things. As ***Colossians 1:16-17*** declares, ***"For by him were all things created, that are in heaven, and that are in earth, visible and invisible, whether they be thrones, or dominions, or principalities, or powers: all things were created by him, and for him. And he is before all things, and by him all things consist."*** Just think about it: you can own vehicles, properties, businesses, etc., but who is the owner of those things? How is it that we, as human beings made lower than the Angels **(Psalms 8:5),** are considered owners of the things on this earth but do not consider who owns us, the mystery of the metaphysical, which is beyond our comprehension? If we as humans do not humble ourselves and recognize that there is a mastermind behind who we are, where we are living, and how we are being preserved, then we are fools as **Psalms 14: 1** says, **"The fool hath said in his heart, There is no God."**

Evidence that there is a God

Some people have several excuses for thinking God isn't real. Usually, they make assertions like, where is God? I don't hear, see, or feel Him. Most people will question the existence of God due to feeling abandoned, especially when they are going through some trials in their lives. However, our inability to see or touch God doesn't make Him non-existent. God is so many things. He is eternal, meaning He possesses an infinite life that is without beginning or end (see Isaiah 40:28). God is immutable (unchanging), He is omnipresent (ever-present), He is omnipotent (all powerful), He is omniscient (knows all) He is all this and more, however, non-existent isn't one of them.

If you believe in the word of God and have received the revelation that the Bible isn't a regular book, then you can examine His word to bring the truth about His existence.

Understanding God Exists Through Creation

Romans 1:20 declares, ***"For* the invisible things of him from the creation *of the world are clearly seen, being understood by the things that are made even by his eternal power and Godhead; so they are without excuse."***

That verse emphasises that the creation of this world gives us a reason to believe that there is God, and it reveals a power of extensive design that we cannot explain. When we look around and see nature, the living things, sun, moon, stars, clouds, and rain that comes and goes. How do we explain all of that? His words are saying that our inability to explain and fathom the world we live in and how it operates without an operator being visible and present proves that there is a higher being working behind the scene.

The handyman is God. Genesis 1:1 state that "***In the beginning God created the heaven and the earth."***

Psalms 19:1 continues by saying, **T*he heavens declare his glory and the firmament shows his handy work.'*** Paul wrote to the Romans saying they have no excuse; we have no excuse not to believe in God. Let's retain this knowledge of God and reverse ***Romans 1: 28.*** It says in ***Romans 1:21 that when they knew God they glorified him not as God, neither were they thankful… 22, professing themselves to be wise, they became fools.***

God has given us enough visible proof shows His invisible power and scriptures which declare this truth. Scriptures such as ***1 Timothy 1:17, Colossians 1:16-17, Psalms 104:5,*** and ***Revelation 4:11***.

We can't see God nor touch Him; therefore, we need faith to understand that the world was created by a higher being. Hebrews 11:3 states, "***Through faith, we understand that the worlds were framed by the word of God, so that things which are seen were not made of things which do appear.'***

Remember, "***The Lord by wisdom hath founded the earth; by understanding hath established the heavens" Proverbs 3:19.*** *And* ***"In the beginning God created heaven and the earth" Genesis 1:1.*** He made the earth and everything in it in six days and rested on the seventh. The first man God made was "Adam," and he was moulded and ***formed by God from the dust of the earth; the Lord then breathed into his nostrils the breath of life and he***

(Adam) became a living soul. God then thought of making a helper for Adam; for in his eye, it was not good for Adam to be alone. So he made women by causing a deep sleep to fall upon Adam and he took one of his ribs and closed up the flesh. He used that very rib to make the woman (Eve). Think about that for a moment… I encourage you to read ***Genesis chapters 1 and 2*** to understand how the earth and everything in it was created.

Understanding God Exists Through Moral Law

My question to you is this: How do we distinguish between what is wrong and right or bad and good? Where did the aspect of distinguishing right from wrong come from? How did it come about, and where did it come from? How do we know that we ought to be good people, and why does being bad leave an abhorrent taste in our mouths? Another question: how did sin became sin? Who calls sin—sin? Firstly, what is a sin to begin with? According to the Oxford dictionary, "Sin is an immoral act considered to be a transgression against divine law." To clearly understand this, let's define the term law. "Law is the system of rules which a particular country or community recognizes as regulating the actions of its members and which it may enforce by the imposition of penalties." (Oxford Dictionary)

The Bible concurs with the above definition, or shall I say Google and the Oxford dictionary concur with what the Bible says because the Bible was established way before Google and dictionaries. Let's observe the few scriptures of the Apostle Paul:

Romans 5:13 ***"For until the law sin was in the world: but sin is not imputed when there is no law."***

Romans 7:7 ***"What shall we say then? Is the law sin? God forbid. Nay, I had not known sin, but by the law: for I had not known lust, except the law had said, thou shalt not covet."***

Romans 7:12 "Wherefore the law is holy, and the commandment holy, and just, and good."

Romans 7:16 "If then I do that which I would not, I consent unto the law that it is good."

In Romans 7, Paul was bringing awareness to the fact that believers are not made holy by the law but by God's Grace. However, he wanted to shed light on the essence of the law. The law he speaks of is the first set of laws ever given to a set of people who Moses led. This is where it all began. Law was first introduced more than three thousand years ago, although God gave Adam and Eve His first commandment in **Genesis 2:16-17**. However, with Moses, this is where the first set of laws were established and given to a set of people. Also, consequences were given when the laws were broken. Who gave those consequences? God Himself punished those who broke the first law he gave to Moses for the people on mount Sina, which says, ***"Thou shalt have no other Gods before me" Exodus 20:3***

In chapter 32 of Exodus, the people transgressed against the divine law from Heaven.

Exodus 32:2-4

"And Aaron said unto them, Break off the golden earrings, which are in the ears of your wives, of your sons, and of your daughters, and bring them unto me. And all the people brake off the golden earrings which were in their ears, and brought them unto Aaron. And he received them at their hand, and

fashioned it with a graving tool, after he had made it a molten calf: and they said, These be thy gods, O Israel, which brought thee up out of the land of Egypt."

Here in ***Exodus 32:21,*** Moses calls it sin: ***"And Moses said unto Aron, what did this people unto thee, that thou hast brought so great a sin upon them."***

Here in ***Exodus 32:27, the*** penalty was enforced for disobeying the law, ***"And he said unto them, Thus saith the LORD God of Israel, Put every man his sword by his side, and go in and out from gate to gate throughout the camp, and slay every man his brother, and every man his companion, and every man his neighbour."***

We know where law and sin were derived from. The essence of moral law and moral value stems from our creator, in whose image and likeness we are made. That code of ethics is embedded in our DNA because that is who Christ is; He is good, honest, faithful, loving, forgiving, fair, selfless, righteous, and perfect. However, He has given us liberty. "**For, brethren, ye have been called unto liberty; only use not liberty**

for an occasion to the flesh, but by love serve one another" Galatians 5:13.

The freedom of choice! We get to decide whether to do what is right or wrong. Righteousness comes from the spirit of the living God, and we all have the spirit of Christ living inside of us ***1 Corinthians 3:16.*** That is where the knowledge and feeling stems from. Knowing what is right helps to understand what is the antithesis of it. It is the good that helps us to know what is wrong. God is that good. Moral law demands a law-giver, and that's God. **Isaiah 33:22 says, "*For the LORD is our judge, the LORD is our lawgiver, the LORD is our king; he will save us.*"** and there is only one lawgiver in heaven and earth. **James 4:12 "*There is one lawgiver, who is able to save and to destroy: who art thou that judgest another?*"** If there is no God, then it's not wrong to do what is wrong, and there is no wrong; however; if there is a God and he loves what's good and hates what is evil, then there must be a moral code embedded in our hearts. Let's observe the scriptures that speak of God's law being embedded in the hearts of His people.

Jeremiah 31:33 "…I will put my law in their inward parts, and write it in their hearts; and will be their God, and they shall be my people."

Hebrews 8:10 "For this is the covenant that I will make with the house of Israel after those days, saith the Lord; I will put my laws into their mind, and write them in their hearts: and I will be to them a God, and they shall be to me a people:"

Hebrews 10:16 "This is the covenant that I will make with them after those days, saith the Lord, I will put my laws into their hearts, and in their minds will I write them"

Romans 2:15 "Which shew the work of the law written in their hearts, their conscience also bearing witness, and their thoughts the mean while accusing or else excusing one another"

We show the essential requirement of the law by displaying moral values of doing what is right and knowing what is wrong. It is our heart that shows a reflection of the law. **Romans 3:16** says **"In the day when God shall judge the secrets of men by Jesus Christ according to my gospel." This means that God is the judge, and when He judges, He will look**

at the heart of men and expose their deepest secrets."

Understanding God Exists Through Experience

Experience is defined as the fact or state of having been affected by or gained knowledge through direct observation or participation. (Merriam-Webster, 2019)

Some will never believe that God exists unless they have a personal encounter with Him or witness the move of God in someone's life. Just like Saul, before he was Paul, didn't believe in Jesus as Lord until he had a personal experience with him near Damascus. (Acts 9:3-8) The following gives us an insight into how kings and people acknowledged the true and living God through experiences.

Elijah on Mount Carmel: Jehovah versus Baal

Elijah contended with Ahab concerning the true and living God. The two concluded that they would experiment by calling upon their Gods. Whoever God answers by fire would have proven to be the true and living God. Ahab had influenced the people to serve a false god called Baal. However, Elijah desired the people to know that Ahab's god was powerless and that the people should be serving the true God. Both men chose a bullock and dressed it. Ahab went first; they called on the name of Baal from morning to evening and got no response. They even cut themselves until blood was shed, and still no reply (1 Kings 18:25-29). Elijah then proceeds to call upon his God; however, prior to calling upon God, he drenched the altar with water. 1 Kings 18:38 declares, "***Then the fire of the LORD fell, and consumed the burnt sacrifice, and the wood, and the stones, and the dust, and licked up the water that was in the trench.***" The people were able to experience the move of God, and it resulted in them believing and turning to God. ***1 Kings 18:39 "And when all the people saw it, they fell on their faces: and they said, The Lord, he is the God; the Lord, he is the God."***

King Nebuchadnezzar's Dream Revealed: Daniel Interprets It

After Juda was besieged by the Babylonians, King Nebuchadnezzar, as the reigning king, dreamed. He called for the magicians and astrologers to recall his dream, as he didn't remember it, and to provide the interpretation thereof. None of them could perform the task. In fact, they claim it to be impossible by any man upon the earth ***Daniel 2:10*** and stated that it's a rare thing that the king has requested ***Daniel 2:11.*** Their inability to deliver led the King to command that all astrologers, magicians, and wise men be put to death. Daniel heard of the command and requested time to seek his God and deliver upon the King's request. **Daniel 2:19** says, ***"Then was the secret revealed unto Daniel in a night vision. Then Daniel blessed the God of heaven."*** Daniel recalled the dream the king could no longer remember and interpreted it to the King. When Daniel concluded his interpretation, the King promoted him. He responded in **Daniel 2:**47, saying, ***"Of a truth it is, that your God is a God of gods, and a Lord of kings, and a revealer of secrets, seeing thou couldest reveal this secret."***

The evidence of Daniel's God was visible. What the Chaldeans thought was impossible, God made it possible. When they considered it a rare thing, God specialised in that rare thing.

The King's experience resulted in him believing in the true and living God. The king expected the impossible from the astrologers. In that spirit of expectancy; he unlocked a faith in himself that resulted in God doing the uncommon, the rare, the impossible in the life of Daniel.

In that, God was Glorified, and the king had an experience.

The First Apostolic Miracle: The Lame Healed

Peter and John were on their way to the temple at the hour of prayer. As they approached the gate of the temple called Beautiful, they saw a man lame from his mother's womb. This man was begging for something to sustain himself. Peter and John responded with a Miracle; in ***Acts 3:6, "Then Peter said, Silver and gold have I none: but such as I have give I thee: in the name of Jesus Christ of Nazareth rise up and walk."*** Peter then took the lame man up by the right hand, and immediately his feet and ankle bones received strength ***(Acts 3:7)***. This lame man experienced the power of God in his life; this resulted in him praising God ***(Acts 3:8).*** Being lame from his mother's womb, he was known as the lame man in the neighbourhood. Everyone knew him as that, so when the people witnessed him as the antithesis to what they knew him to be: walking, leaping, and praising God, they were filled with wonder and amazement ***(Acts 3:10)***. This then indicated that they were witnessed unto the lame man's experience. His experience left an impact on them. Because of how they responded to the miracle that transpired, Peter seized that opportunity to highlight God for the cause. In Peter's exhortation to the people, the high priest and captain of the temple were grieved and managed to apprehend them in an attempt to prevent them from preaching the resurrection of Jesus from the dead. Nevertheless, Acts *4:4* declares that ***"Howbeit many of them who heard the word believed; and the number of the men was about five thousand."*** This lame man's experience resulted in thousands of people knowing the God of miracles.

There are many other stories in the Bible where people encountered God. Their personal experiences made them understand that God, indeed, does exist. Especially when they can't seem to find any critical answer to the experiences they have encountered. Have you ever had an encounter with the Holy Spirit? Have you ever cried out to God for help and he answered you in unusual ways? Have you ever witnessed the move of God in someone's life that led you to believe, "This must have been God that did it?" Have you?

We go through life experiencing the inexperienced. We all have personal encounters and can testify of an extraordinary thing that transpired with unbelievable explanations. Can any of those experiences help you to understand that there is a living God? I encourage you to reminisce, take this time to reflect, and dig up old or current memories of situations that occurred in your life. Give God the Glory. He deserves it.

Understanding God Exists Through Faith

Now faith is something I can't explain; no one can explain; however, the Bible states perfectly in Hebrews 11:1, ***"Now faith is the substance of things hoped for, the evidence of things not seen."*** Faith is everything we need to believe that God exists. Firstly, we have never seen God, so it takes faith to believe that He even exists. Secondly, it takes faith for us to believe in the process of how the earth came to be. Not a living soul on earth can ever say they have witnessed this earth being formed. ***"Through faith we understand that the worlds were framed by the word of God, so that things which are seen were not made of things which do appear." Hebrews 11:3*** The earth was here before you and I were; we just accept that this is where we should abode and live. We have been exercising faith since the day we were born.

Why should it be hard to accept that there is a God through faith? Do you know how blessed we are when we exercise faith in believing in the one true and living God without seeing Him? John 20:28 says, ***"Jesus saith unto him, Thomas, because thou hast seen me, thou hast believed: blessed are they that have not seen, and yet have believed."***

Glory to God! It takes a level of faith to believe in a God whom we have not seen. I would rather be a part of the people who have chosen to believe that there is God rather than not believing. Let us not take on the spirit of doubt attributed to Thomas, but choose to believe in a higher being than ourselves, choose to believe that there is a creator of this world, choose to believe that you have a creator, choose to believe that there is a God that does miracles, choose to believe that there is a God that loves you, choose to believe in the blessed hope, and choose to believe that there is a God to depend on and trust in. Let our faith continue to stand in God's power and not that of men (***1 Corinthians 2:5***).

Here are a few scriptures for your reading that acknowledge those who applied faith. I hope you understand the way of faith through the many heroes of faith.

Hebrews 11:4-40

4 By faith Abel offered unto God a more excellent sacrifice than Cain, by which he obtained witness that he was righteous, God testifying of his gifts: and by it he being dead yet speaketh.

5 By faith Enoch was translated that he should not see death; and was not found, because God had translated him: for before his translation he had this testimony, that he pleased God.

6 But without faith it is impossible to please him: for he that cometh to God must believe that he is, and that he is a rewarder of them that diligently seek him.

7 By faith Noah, being warned of God of things not seen as yet, moved with fear, prepared an ark to the saving of his house; by the which he condemned the world, and became heir of the righteousness which is by faith.

8 By faith Abraham, when he was called to go out into a place which he should after receive for an

inheritance, obeyed; and he went out, not knowing whither he went.

9 By faith he sojourned in the land of promise, as in a strange country, dwelling in tabernacles with Isaac and Jacob, the heirs with him of the same promise:

10 For he looked for a city which hath foundations, whose builder and maker is God.

11 Through faith also Sara herself received strength to conceive seed, and was delivered of a child when she was past age, because she judged him faithful who had promised.

12 Therefore sprang there even of one, and him as good as dead, so many as the stars of the sky in multitude, and as the sand which is by the sea shore innumerable.

13 These all died in faith, not having received the promises, but having seen them afar off, and were persuaded of them, and embraced them, and confessed that they were strangers and pilgrims on the earth.

14 For they that say such things declare plainly that they seek a country.

15 And truly, if they had been mindful of that country from whence they came out, they might have had opportunity to have returned.

16 But now they desire a better country, that is, an heavenly: wherefore God is not ashamed to be called their God: for he hath prepared for them a city.

17 By faith Abraham, when he was tried, offered up Isaac: and he that had received the promises offered up his only begotten son,

18 Of whom it was said, That in Isaac shall thy seed be called:

19 Accounting that God was able to raise him up, even from the dead; from whence also he received him in a figure.

20 By faith Isaac blessed Jacob and Esau concerning things to come.

21 By faith Jacob, when he was dying, blessed both the sons of Joseph; and worshipped, leaning upon the top of his staff.

22 By faith Joseph, when he died, made mention of the departing of the children of Israel; and gave commandment concerning his bones.

23 By faith Moses, when he was born, was hid three months of his parents, because they saw he was a proper child; and they were not afraid of the king's commandment.

24 By faith Moses, when he was come to years, refused to be called the son of Pharaoh's daughter;

25 Choosing rather to suffer affliction with the people of God, than to enjoy the pleasures of sin for a season;

26 Esteeming the reproach of Christ greater riches than the treasures in Egypt: for he had respect unto the recompence of the reward.

27 By faith he forsook Egypt, not fearing the wrath of the king: for he endured, as seeing him who is invisible.

28 Through faith he kept the passover, and the sprinkling of blood, lest he that destroyed the firstborn should touch them.

29 By faith they passed through the Red sea as by dry land: which the Egyptians assaying to do were drowned.

30 By faith the walls of Jericho fell down, after they were compassed about seven days.

31 By faith the harlot Rahab perished not with them that believed not, when she had received the spies with peace.

32 And what shall I more say? for the time would fail me to tell of Gedeon, and of Barak, and of Samson, and of Jephthae; of David also, and Samuel, and of the prophets:

33 Who through faith subdued kingdoms, wrought righteousness, obtained promises, stopped the mouths of lions.

34 Quenched the violence of fire, escaped the edge of the sword, out of weakness were made strong, waxed valiant in fight, turned to flight the armies of the aliens.

35 Women received their dead raised to life again: and others were tortured, not accepting deliverance; that they might obtain a better resurrection:

36 And others had trial of cruel mockings and scourgings, yea, moreover of bonds and imprisonment:

37 They were stoned, they were sawn asunder, were tempted, were slain with the sword: they wandered about in sheepskins and goatskins; being destitute, afflicted, tormented;

38 (Of whom the world was not worthy:) they wandered in deserts, and in mountains, and in dens and caves of the earth.

39 And these all, having obtained a good report through faith, received not the promise:

40 God having provided some better thing for us, that they without us should not be made perfect.

QUESTION 3

Is there one God?

Deuteronomy 6:4 declares, ***'Hear O Israel; the Lord Our God is one God.'*** No three persons can be in charge. If God threw Lucifer out of heaven ***(Isaiah 14:12)*** because he wanted to rule and take charge, why would we think there is more than one God? As a mere human, I find it quite difficult to comprehend the fullness of God.

He is unfathomable:

He is Elohim: The Supreme one or Mighty one (***Genesis 1:1***)

He is El Roi: The God who sees me (***Genesis 16:13***)

He is El Shaddai: God Almighty (***Genesis 17:1)***

He is Jehovah Jireh: The Lord our Provider (***Genesis 22:14***)

He is Jehovah Rapha: The Lord our Healer ***(Exodus 15:26)***

He *is* Jehovah Nissi: The Lord our Banner ***(Exodus 17:15)***

He is Jehovah Shalom: The Lord our Peace ***(Judges 6:24)***

He is *Jehovah Rohi****:*** The Lord our Shepherd ***(Psalm 23:1)***

He is Jehovah Tsidkenu: The Lord our Righteousness **(Jeremiah *23:6)***

Just as God is able to be all of the above when so ever, he desires. God can be one and still be three different things whilst maintaining his fullness. However, this doesn't mean that there are three Gods, but rather there is one powerful God that can become whomever He desires and wherever He desires. In the Bible, we notice mention of the Father, the Son, and the Holy Spirit ***(Matthew 28:19).*** This speaks of God being three in one; in the former section of that verse, it says, "In the name." It's the name of one God, revealing himself in three different forms for the betterment of his creation.

He is Father in creation, Son in redemption, and the Holy Spirit in the church. Let's examine God in all three to observe the unity evident and how He is one, in essence, three in person.

FATHER IN CREATION

Genesis 1:1 "In the beginning God created the heaven and the earth."

Colossians 1:16

"For by him were all things created, that are in heaven, and that are in earth, visible and invisible, whether they be thrones, or dominions, or principalities, or powers: all things were created by him, and for him:"

John 1:3

"All things were made by him; and without him there was not anything made that was made."

Malachi 2:10

"Have we not all one father? Hath not God created us? Why do we deal treacherously every man

against his brother, by profaning the covenant of our fathers"

Isaiah 63:16 "Doubtless thou art our father, though Abraham be ignorant of us, and Israel acknowledge us not: thou, O LORD, art our father, our redeemer; thy name is from everlasting."

Isaiah 64:8 "But now, O LORD, thou art our father; we are the clay, and thou our potter; and we all are the work of thy hand."

Acts 17:28 "For in him we live, and move, and have our being; as certain also of your own poets have said, For we are also his offspring."

Matthew 6:9 "After this manner therefore pray ye: Our Father which art in heaven, Hallowed be thy name."

Son in redemption

Matthew 1:21 "And she shall bring forth a son, and thou shalt call his name JESUS: for he shall save his people from their sins."

Ephesians 1:7 "In whom we have redemption through his blood, the forgiveness of sins, according to the riches of his grace;"

Hebrews 9:12 "Neither by the blood of goats and calves, but by his own blood he entered once into the holy place, having obtained eternal redemption for us."

Galatians 3:13 "Christ hath redeemed us from the curse of the law, being made a curse for us: for it is written, Cursed is everyone that hangeth on a tree:"

Psalm 103:4 "Who redeemeth thy life from destruction; who crowneth thee with lovingkindness and tender mercies;"

Titus 2:14 "Who gave himself for us, that he might redeem us from all iniquity, and purify unto himself a peculiar people, zealous of good works."

Holy Spirt in the Church/in Us

Genesis 1:2 "And the earth was without form, and void; and darkness was upon the face of the deep. And the Spirit of God moved upon the face of the waters."

Genesis 6:3 "And the LORD said, My spirit shall not always strive with man, for that he also is flesh: yet his days shall be an hundred and twenty years."

John 4:24 "God is a Spirit: and they that worship him must worship him in spirit and in truth."

2 Corinthians 3:17 "Now the Lord is that Spirit: and where the Spirit of the Lord is, there is liberty."

Psalm 139:7 "Whither shall I go from thy spirit? or whither shall I flee from thy presence?"

John 14:16-17 "And I will pray the father, and he shall give you another Comforter, that he may abide with you forever; Even the spirit of truth; whom the world cannot receive, because it seeth him

not, neither knoweth him: but ye know him; for he dwelleth with you, and shall be in you."

Jesus is Lord

In ***Matthew 28:19 where it states, "Go ye therefore, and teach all nations, baptizing them in the name of the Father, and of the Son, and of the Holy Ghost."***

The name being referred to here is Jesus. Jesus Christ of Nazareth, the Son of God. Lord in the form of Son in Redemption. There is one God and Lord, and that is Jesus. When Saul encountered God in Acts 9, he asked this question; "Who art thou, Lord? And the Lord replied by saying, I am Jesus whom thou persecutest: it is hard for thee to kick against the pricks."

Only God can forgive sins:

Mark 2:5 "When Jesus saw their faith, he said unto the sick of the palsy, Son thy sins be forgiven."

Mark 2:10 "But that ye may know that the son of man hath power on earth to forgive sins, (he saith to the sick palsy).

Luke 24: 47 "And that repentance and remission of sins should be preached in his name among all nations, beginning at Jerusalem."

Only God can resurrect from the dead:

Mark 16:6 "And he saith unto them, Be not affrighted: Ye seek Jesus of Nazareth, which was crucified: he is risen; he is not here: behold the place where they laid him."

Mark 16:9 "Now when Jesus was risen early the first day of the week, he appeared first to Mary Magdalene, out of whom he had cast seven devils."

Luke 24:34 "Saying, The Lord is risen indeed, and hath appeared to Simon.

Luke 24:39 "Behold my hands and my feet, that it is I myself: handle me, and see; for a spirit hath not flesh and bones, as ye see me have."

Luke 24:46 "And said unto them, Thus it is written, and thus it behoved Christ to suffer, and to rise from the dead the third day:"

Corinthians 15:4 "And that he was buried, and that he rose again the third day according to scriptures."

Only God has All the Powers:

Matthew 28:18 "And Jesus came and spoke unto them, saying, All power is given unto me in heaven and in earth.

John 10:18 "No man taketh it from me, but I lay it down myself. I have power to lay it down, and I have power to take it again. This commandment I have received of my Father."

Philippians 2:10 "That at the name of Jesus every knee should bow, of things in heaven, and things in earth, and things under the earth;"

Only God Can Give Eternal Life:

John 10:28 "And I give unto them eternal life; and they shall never perish, neither shall any man pluck them out of my hand."

Romans 6:23 "For the wages of sin is death; but the gift of God is eternal life through Jesus Christ our Lord."

1 John 5:11-12 "And this is the record, that God hath given to us eternal life, and this life is in his Son. He that hath the Son hath life; and he that hath not the Son of God hath not life."

Jesus was declared Lord by Elizabeth the mother of John the Baptist , before he was even birthed into this world. ***Luke 1:43 "And whence is this to me, that the mother of my Lord should come to me?"*** Paul mentioned Jesus as Lord by saying, ***"But other of the apostles saw I none, save James the Lord's brother" in Galatians 1:9.*** Jesus referred to himself as Lord in John 15:20 by saying, ***"Remember the word that I said unto you, The servant is not greater than his lord. If they have persecuted me, they will also persecute you; if they have kept my saying, they will keep yours also."*** In other instances, Jesus mentions how He was with God before the world came into existence. ***"And now, O Father, glorify thou me with thine own self with the glory which I had with thee before the world was." (John 17:5)***

Jesus says ***in John 10:30, "I and my father are one."*** He also says in ***John 17:21*** that the Father is in Him; ***"That they all may be one; as thou, Father, art***

in me, and I in thee, that they also may be one in us: that the world may believe that thou hast sent me."

In John 14:8-9 Phillip called Jesus, Lord, and asked that they be shown who is the Father. Jesus responded by saying, "***Have I been so long time with you, and yet hast thou not known me, Philip? he that hath seen me hath seen the Father; and how sayest thou then, Show us the Father?*** Jesus ends His reply in verses 10 and 11 by saying, ***"Believest thou not that I am in the Father, and the Father in me? the words that I speak unto you I speak not of myself: but the Father that dwelleth in me, he doeth the works. Believe me that I am in the Father, and the Father in me: or else believe me for the very works' sake."***

While we aim to understand everything as mere human beings. Our inability to comprehend our Lord and how He operates should signify deity and supremacy. We shouldn't expect our God to be like us. Him in all, His glory, and power is what distinguishes Him from mortal beings like us. To know that He was able to descend from heaven and abode with us to accomplish a goal to save humanity. It gives me peace in knowing that I have a Lord who is willing and able to do anything for the sake of His people. ***Philippians 2:6-8*** says, ***"Who, being in the form of God, thought it not robbery to be equal with God: But made himself of no reputation, and took upon him the form of a servant, and was made in the likeness of men: And being found in fashion as a man, he humbled himself, and became obedient unto death, even the death of the cross."***

Who wouldn't believe that Jesus is Lord? One day we all will have to confess that Jesus Christ is Lord ***(Philippians 2:11)***

And the LORD shall be king over all the earth: in that day shall there be one LORD, and his name one.

Zechariah 14: 9

QUESTION 4

How do I get saved?

This question comes from a curious individual, who has been contemplating giving their life to Christ. Some people are confused with religion, church, God, life after death, heaven, hell, right, wrong, etc. Confusion is a breathing ground for a lack of decision-making. How this question is answered can either prolong their decision to give their life to Christ or be an immediate open door to them saying yes to Jesus.

I want to insert this scripture before I go in-depth to answer this question. Paul says in ***Acts 4:12, "Neither is there salvation in any other: for there is none other name under heaven given among men, whereby we must be saved."***

Salvation comes from the word "saved," hence, it's paramount to know who our salvation comes from, and Paul made sure to enlighten us on this. Let's observe the previous verses to Acts 4:12. Acts 4:10-11 says

"Be ***it known unto you all, and to all the people of Israel, that by the name of Jesus Christ of Nazareth whom ye crucified, whom God raised from the dead, even by him doth this man stand here before you whole. This is the stone which was set at nought of you builders, which has become the head of the corner."***

In the previous chapter, a Lame man was healed by Peter and John. This man was at the gate of a temple called Beautiful. The story is that he had been lame since his mother's womb and had stayed at the entrance of the temple; so, whoever entered, he asked for charitable deeds. While Peter and John were about to enter the temple, he asked them for alms, and this was Peter's response, ***"Silver and gold have I none; but such as I have give I thee: In the name of Jesus Christ of Nazareth rise up and walk." Acts 3:6.***

After this notable miracle, people started praising God. They were filled with wonder and amazement at what had been done. Peter ensured that he gave all the glory to God. Acts 3:12-13: ***"And when Peter saw it, he answered unto the people, ye men of Israel, why marvel ye at this? Or why look ye so earnestly on us, as though by our own power or***

holiness we had made this man to walk? The God of Abraham, and of Isaac, and of Jacob, the God of our fathers, hath glorified his son Jesus: whom ye delivered up, and denied him in the presence of Pilate, when he was determined to let him go."

Peter then gave his exhortation on repentance and preached the resurrection from the dead through Jesus. As he and John spoke, the people who heard the word; believed. However, the Sadducees were grieved, and they put them away until the next day. This was the first persecution. Peter and John were then released, and they were asked by the rulers, elders, etc., "B***y what power, or by what name, have ye done this?"*** The "this" he was referring to was the healing of the lame man. This is where ***Acts 4: 10-11*** came in. Peter was making it known unto everyone that it was by Jesus Christ of Nazareth, whom they crucified, who God raised from the dead, that the impotent man was made whole. The one whom they rejected had become the one they needed for everything, including salvation. Peter then explains in **Acts 4:12** that our salvation comes from Jesus Christ alone; we can only be saved through Him. ***Matthew 1:21*** declares ***"And she shall bring forth a son, and***

thou shalt call his name Jesus: for he shall save his people from their sins."

I've come to the conclusion that there are six steps we ought to go through to get saved.

1. **HEAR THE WORD**
2. **BELIEVE IN JESUS (DEATH, BURIAL, RESURRECTION)**
3. **REPENT OF SINS**
4. **CONFESS YOUR FAITH**
5. **BE BAPTIZED**
6. **BE TRANSFORMED THROUGH THE WORD**

HEAR THE WORD OF GOD

Firstly, we must hear the word of God to know in whom we will put our faith. **Romans 10:17** declares, ***"So then faith comes by hearing and hearing by the word of God."***

I'd like to share instances in the Bible where the word of God was preached and taught, and people who listened believed and gave their lives to Christ.

Acts 2:37 says, "***Now when they heard this, they were pricked in their hearts, and said unto Peter and to the rest of apostles, men and brethren, what shall we do?"***

This was Peter's first use of the gospel, and he was exhorting the people. In the previous verses, he sheds light on how the resurrection proves that Jesus is Lord and Christ. I encourage you to read the entire chapter for yourself.

In Peter's obedience to teaching the word of God, the people's hearts were pricked. They were touched by the gospel. It's imperative to give people the opportunity to experience this, to hear the word, and let it pierce their hearts. Hebrews 4:12 says, "***For the word of God is quick and powerful, and sharper than any twoedged sword, piercing even to the dividing asunder of soul and spirit, and of the joints***

and marrow, and is a discerner of the thoughts and intents of the heart.

Yes, that's what the power of the word of God alone can do. No one needs to be compelled, forced, or even feared into accepting Jesus as their Lord and Saviour. People first need to receive the word and obtain faith in what they have heard. Once they have been touched by the gospel, they will eventually ask for the next step. Just as in Acts 2:37, the people asked, "***What shall we do?***" Their pricked hearts will spark curiosity in knowing how to get saved and give their life to Christ. Although, some will immediately believe and give their life to Christ.

Acts 11:19-21 says, "***Now they which were scattered abroad upon the persecution that arose about Stephen travelled as far as Phenice, and Cyprus, and Antioch preaching the word to none but unto the Jews only. 20*And some of them were men of Cyprus and Cyrene, which, when they came to Antioch, spoke unto the Grecians, preaching the Lord Jesus. 21* And the hand of the Lord was with them: and a great number believed, and turned unto the Lord.***"

Let's take note of one of the few people in the Bible who were curious about the next steps in accepting Jesus as Lord and Saviour or who asked, "What must I do to be saved?"

In Acts 16, Paul had a vision of a man from Macedonia. In that vision, this man was praying, saying, "Come over into Macedonia, and help us." The vision led Paul to travel to Macedonia to preach the gospel. On that journey, he visited multiple cities, and when he got to Phillipi, he baptised a woman named Lydia and her household. He then delivered another lady who was possessed with the spirit of divination. Through the manifestation of the power of God in Paul's life, people began to believe and were open to receiving the way of salvation. I want to interject here and say that some people will believe and expediently give their life over to Christ only when they witness the power of God. For Jesus, Himself says in ***John 4:48, "Except ye see signs and wonders, ye will not believe."*** Hence why it's essential that women and men of God maintain their relationship with Him so that their growth in Him can be one in which His power is evident in their lives. The souls of people depend on it. Although we are not responsible for saving people, we are expected to plant the seed, allow another to water it, and allow God to give the increase. Paul says this in 1 Corinthians 3:6 ***"I have planted, Apollos watered; but God gave the increase."***

Although some people believed in the miracles done by the hand of Paul, some were displeased with his intervention in the life of the damsel whom he made whole. The power of God being manifested interrupted the business of the masters whom the damsel went to for deliverance as she spent money to be whole. Basically, Paul's presence and God's power ran them out of their deceptive business. This led the masters to bring Paul and Silas to the magistrates. It was reported that Paul and Silas were troubling their city and teaching customs that weren't lawful for them to receive. They rose against Paul and Silas, beat them, and they were then put into prison. Paul and Silas sang praises to God at midnight in the prison, and the power of God was manifested; so much that there was an earthquake. Immediately, all the prison doors were opened, and everyone was no longer in bondage. The residing verses of **Acts 16** talk of the interaction between the Philippian jailor and Paul and Silas. In verse 30, the gatekeeper (jailor) asks, ***"What must I do to be saved?"*** Paul and Silas' response brings me to our second step of getting saved. **Acts 16:31** declares, ***"And they said, Believe on the Lord Jesus Christ, and thou shalt be saved, and thy house."*** The word was written that we may believe and have life through Jesus's name alone. Provide an opportunity to hear God's word. Rather from an anointed preacher or teacher, or by reading the word of God personally. **John 20:31** says, ***"But these were written that ye might believe that Jesus is the Christ, the son of God; and that believing ye might have life through his name."*** This now brings us to the second step in getting saved: "Believing in the Gospel"

BELIEVE IN JESUS (DEATH, BURIAL, RESURRECTION)

To believe means to accept something is true without proof. We are required to believe in a God we haven't seen. Just because we haven't witnessed something doesn't make it untrue or unworthy of believing. When a person is put on trial, the judge and the jury have to determine whether that person is guilty based on the probative nature of the evidence before the court or statements from witnesses. The judge and jury didn't witness the actions caused by the person on trial, yet they had to believe in the witnesses or evidence presented. From the evidence and testimony of the witnesses, they believe and conclude how to reprimand the victim. Justice is then served.

J*ohn 20:29 says, "Jesus saith unto him, Thomas, because thou hast seen me, thou hast believed: blessed are they that have not seen, and yet have believed."* You are considered blessed if you believe without witnessing. The disciples witnessed the manifestation of the gospel, and it was written for us to believe in what they have witnessed.

J*ohn 20:31 says, "But these are written, that ye might believe that Jesus is the Christ, the Son of God; and that believing ye might have life through his name."*

Life comes from believing in the above. It's required by us to believe in the Gospel: the death, burial, and resurrection of Jesus Christ of Nazareth.

1 Corinthians 15: 14 "Moreover, brethren, I declare unto you the gospel which I preached unto you, which also ye have received, and wherein ye stand; By which also ye are saved, if ye keep in memory what I preached unto you, unless ye have

believed in vain. For I delivered unto you first of all that which I also received, how that Christ died for our sins according to the scriptures; And that he was buried, and that he rose again the third day according to the scriptures: And that he was seen of Cephas, then of the twelve."

Jesus's death, burial, and resurrection was witnessed. There was evidence, and there were witnesses. Those witnesses testified verbally in ancient times and left a hard copy of their testimony so those coming after them would have something to believe in. Can you believe in the gospel? Can you believe that Jesus Christ died for you and me? Can you believe that this same Jesus rose from the dead? Can you believe that only through Jesus Christ of Nazareth can you be saved? All you have to do is believe. If you believe, nothing will be subtracted from your life, but it's a fact there is a blessed hope in your belief. Your faith will never be in vain. Jesus is the way, the truth, and the life ***John 14:16***. He alone rose from the dead. In ***Acts chapter 1:3,*** Jesus showed Himself to the people after He was resurrected. He stayed with them for forty days and He spoke about the Kingdom of God.

I love how Paul eloquently explained the first resurrection in ***1 Corinthians 15:12-17.*** He was encouraging the people on how Christ did indeed rise from the dead; however, if he didn't truly rise from the dead, then they are false witnesses, and their preaching and faith would be in vain, which means we are still in our sin—no redemption, no salvation! What a life to live. Please read the verses below of Paul expounding on the above scriptures.

"Now if Christ be preached that he rose from the dead, how say some among you that there is no resurrection of the dead? But if there be no resurrection of the dead, then is Christ not risen: And if Christ be not risen, then is our preaching vain, and your faith is also vain. Yea, and we are found false witnesses of God; because we have testified of God that he raised up Christ: whom he raised not up, if so be that the dead rise not. For if the dead rise not, then is not Christ raised: And if Christ be not raised, your faith is vain; ye are yet in your sins."

Know that believing in the gospel is essential to being saved as a child of God. It's through your belief in Jesus' death, burial, and resurrection you are redeemed; you have received power to salvation. Do not be ashamed to accept Jesus' ultimate sacrifice for you. "***For God so loved the world, that he gave his only begotten Son, that whosoever believeth in him should not perish, but have everlasting life." John 3:16***

Paul declares in Romans 1:16, "***For I am not ashamed of the gospel of christ: for it is the power of God unto salvation to everyone that believeth; to the Jews first, and also to the Greek."***

Although believing in the gospel is paramount to being saved, much is still required, and believing is not enough to receive salvation. Hence why Luke says in Mark 16:16, ***"He that believeth and is baptised shall be saved; but he that believeth not shall be damned."*** I passionately adore the fact that there are different stages we ought to go through as children of God. This enables us to choose Christ willingly and allows conversion to take place within us daily. So therefore, once you have believed in the gospel, the step towards your journey to salvation involves being baptised. This brings us to the third, fourth, and fifth steps—all in one, "REPENT, CONFESS, BAPTISM."

Be Baptized

*Acts 2:38 says, "**Then Peter said unto them, Repent, and be baptised every one of you in the name of Jesus Christ for the remission of sins, and ye shall receive the gift of the Holy Ghost.**"* Baptism is a whole different topic to discuss, and it will be explained in more detail in question five. However, let's examine the verse from Peter in the book of Acts. The previous verses talk of those who were pricked in their hearts and have believed; they then proceed to ask Peter what they shall do to be saved. His response in Acts 2:38 encourages them to first REPENT. The term "repent" means to turn away from, change your mind from, or be sorrowful, or remorseful from a bad thing. In this case, it's regarding sin. Firstly, we ought to acknowledge that we are sinners, for David says in Psalm 51, "***Behold, I was shapen in iniquity; and in sin did my mother conceive me.***" *Acknowledging that you have been drowning in sin since you were born is the first step, and confessing your guilt is okay because Jesus came to save us from our sins. Peter says we ought to repent of our sinful ways and be baptised. In addition to repentance, we ought to also confess with our mouths what we believe in. For* **Romans 10:9-10** *declares, "**That if thou confess with***

thy mouth the Lord Jesus, Shalt believe in thine heart that God hath raised him from the dead, thou shalt be saved. For with the heart man believeth unto righteousness; and with the mouth confession is made unto salvation."

More than likely, you will have whomever—whether it is a Pastor, Prophet, Deacon, Elder, or Minister, ask you if you believe that Jesus died for your sins. If you believe that He was raised from the dead? You will then be instructed to confess it with your mouth before either class of the servant of God above decides to baptise you. Before you can be baptised, Repentance and Confession of your faith are the only things that must take place after you have believed in the Lord, Jesus Christ. I have heard of situations where some leaders do not baptise their members unless they have gone through weeks of counselling. I wholeheartedly do not concur with that kind of method. Hence, hearing and allowing the word to convict you into giving your life to Christ is enough. There is nothing anyone can do to counsel you into what the word of God didn't already do. Once your heart has been pricked and you have been convicted, you believe and are ready to take the next step. You are ripe; nothing should prevent you from being baptised. Let's take note of some instances in the Bible, none of which included anyone receiving any counselling before baptism.

Actsc 2: 41 Then they that gladly received his word were baptised: and the same day there were added unto them about three thousand souls.

Acts 8 :12 But when they believed Philip preaching the things concerning the kingdom of God, and the name of Jesus Christ, they were baptised, both men and women.

Acts 8:13 Then Simon himself believed also: and when he was baptised, he continued with Philip, and wondered, beholding the miracles and signs which were done.

Acts 16:14-15 And a certain woman named Lydia, a seller of purple, of the city of Thyatira, which worshipped God, heard us: whose heart the Lord opened, that she attended unto the things which were spoken of Paul. And when she was baptised, and her household, she besought us, saying, If ye have judged me to be faithful to the Lord, come into my house, and abide there. And she constrained us.

Nothing should hinder you from receiving baptism except yourself. You have to want it, you have to need it, and know the purpose of it. Baptism makes you new in Christ by cleansing you from the stain of sin in which you were born. As ***Acts 16:22 declares***

"And now why tarriest thou? arise, and be baptised, and wash away thy sins, calling on the name of the Lord."

Have you believed in the Lord, Jesus Christ? Have you repented of your sins and confessed with your mouth that Jesus Christ is the son of God and that He died and rose from the dead? Are you ready to give your life to Christ? Let me proclaim in your ear that NOTHING hinders you from being baptised at this moment once you have answered yes to the above questions.

Take note of this discussion between Phillip and an Eunuch:

Acts 8:36-38

And as they went on their way, they came unto a certain water: and the eunuch said, See, here is water; what doth hinder me to be baptised?

And Philip said, If thou believest with all thine heart, thou mayest. And he answered and said, I believe that Jesus Christ is the Son of God.

And he commanded the chariot to stand still: and they went down both into the water, both Philip and the eunuch; and he baptised him.

Now that you have been baptised, welcome to the family of God. However, it doesn't end there. This is where the real work commences; this is where you will be tried and tested. This is where your faith will be put to the test. This is where your entire life changes. This is where you have to pray without ceasing, fellowship, worship, and read the word of God. This is where you have to spend time with God. In spending time with God, you will then experience step six (6). You will be transformed if you stay in Christ.

Be Transformed Through The Word

It's actually harder than it sounds. However, transformation is a process, and it doesn't happen overnight. When you desire to be transformed, you ought to be patient with yourself. More importantly, never be too hard on yourself. You will never get it right; it isn't up to you to get it right. You are not transforming yourself, but the word is transforming you. Can you depend on the word to change, mould, and recreate you? Yes, you can. Once you no longer think the same, your desires will change, your attire will change, the way you see yourself and others will change, and the way you speak will never be the same. Only if you allow yourself to be transformed through the word. I beseech you to create room in your heart for the word and to make time for the word. It is the only way to be transformed. When I say the word, I am referring to God himself. As **John 1:1** says, "***In the beginning was the Word, and the Word was with God, and the Word was God.***"

I want to share my personal experience of when I first started being transformed by the word. It was a year after I got baptised. Yes, a year later. In the year 2016, I got baptised. However, I didn't get baptised to serve Christ or become a child of God. I got baptised for the wrong reasons. That year, I found out I had a minor brain tumour, and when I told my roommate about it, she encouraged me to attend her church so that her pastor could pray for me. When I was brought to the front of the altar, he prayed for me. When he concluded his prayer, he spoke about giving my life to Christ, emphasised how only God can heal me, and how God could come at any moment. However, if I wasn't baptised or given my life to Christ, it would be too late, etc. None of what he said made sense to me except the healing part. Because that was what I came to church for—to be healed and set free from a sickness I assume would very well kill me. I have heard of a young individual who died from a brain tumour, and I fret about the sting of death. So being baptised seemed like the ultimate solution to my problem, so, I did it. I do not recall going back to the church after that; I continued with my daily life, work, and college. However, my roommate was a faithful member of the church, and we lived together. So, every now and then, she would invite me to church. I made myself available every once in a while, but I was not committed to going. I only went because she kept asking. Until the frequent visits of hearing the word began to prick my heart, even when my roommate left the country, I continued attending; I didn't know why, but the desire was there. I remember purchasing my very first Bible. I only opened it when I attended church. As time passed, I was curious and convicted in so many ways. I almost felt as though I was being hunted because once I was home alone in the silence, the Bible always came to my mind. Whenever I sensed this urge, I would always open it, although sometimes, I would ignore it or brush it off.

However, one day, I can remember it as clearly as day. I was home alone, and I sat at the dining table and opened the Bible. I finally gave in to that desire. I do not regret it one bit. The day I exercised obedience, it changed my life completely for the better. However, the old me would say "for the worse" as well because my life wasn't the same, and prior to that, I thought my life was going pretty well. I had a waitress job and was making good money. I was in college, I had a boyfriend who treated me exceptionally well, and he made me forget the previous terrible relationship that had me living in fear for years. Let's say my life was well put together; I didn't need anything more, or so I thought. As I continued diving into the word of God, I was constantly being convicted about how I dressed, what I entertained, and even having a boyfriend. My boyfriend used to sleep over most nights, well every night; it didn't matter how late he knocked off from work, he would always find his way over to my house. We were both young adults, and we did adult things and used to enjoy it very much until I started spending time in the word. Our adult encounters didn't feel that enjoyable to me anymore because there was always this sense of guilt within me. There was a hunger for the things of God because those scriptures I read somehow surfaced from nowhere in my thoughts. Flee fornication ***1 Corinthians 6:18,*** do not fulfil the lust of the flesh ***Galatians 5:16,*** do not continue in sin ***Romans 6:1-2,*** sin shall not have dominion over you ***Romans 6:14,*** be holy ***1 Peter 1:16***. I never thought I could remember those scriptures, any scripture for a matter of fact, but God's word is true, and it has power. I am grateful that ***John 14:26*** was evident in my life back then. The comforter was at work for me. He was teaching me, transforming me, bringing to memory everything I had read that was needed in that moment.

"But the Comforter, which is the Holy Ghost, whom the Father will send in my name, he shall teach you all things, and bring all things to your remembrance, whatsoever I have said unto you."

After spending more time with the word, ***Romans 12:2*** started to come alive in me. This is not to say I immediately started living holy and righteous—because that's not what happened. Yes, I eventually broke it off with my boyfriend. Well, I would say I shared my concerns and convictions with him, and he wasn't heading down the path. However, I resolved to take that part, so we agreed to part ways. It was a peaceful breakup; we both still loved and cared for each other. He was still in my life, and so was I. We remained friends but always somehow found ourselves yielding to the flesh. In your walk with Christ, it will take the word of God, the holy spirit, the Father, and the Son to keep you. Yes, I desired to live a holy life, and I tried my best to get it right, but it was a struggle. ***Galatians 5:17*** was evident in my life "***For the flesh lusteth against the Spirit, and the Spirit against the flesh: and these are contrary one to the other: so that ye cannot do the things that ye would.***" I was fighting to do what was right, and although I wanted to do what was right, at some point, I found myself doing what was wrong. In those moments, I could relate to Paul when he said:

"For the good that I would I do not: but the evil which I would not, that I do. Now if I do that I would not, it is no more I that do it, but sin that dwelleth in me. I find then a law, that, when I would do good, evil is present with me. For I delight in the law of God after the inward man: But I see another law in my members, warring against the law of my

mind, and bringing me into captivity to the law of sin which is in my members. O wretched man that I am! Who shall deliver me from the body of this death? I thank God through Jesus Christ our Lord. So then with the mind I myself serve the law of God; but with the flesh the law of sin."

And this is why the first sentence to answer this question was, **"It's actually harder than it sounds."** You don't automatically transform once you get baptised and start living for Christ. It's a process, and it takes time. It may be easier for some, depending on their previous lifestyle. However, it took quite some time for me to be completely transformed. I went through a lot. You may go through a lot, but do not give up. What I can say is that in the season of your life, keep on praying, especially during regretful moments. You can just finish making one of the worst decisions ever, and you feel dirty and filthy, and feel as though you have let God down; you have disappointed Him. You can be in tears; pray with those tears flowing down your cheeks. I promise you a broken and contrite heart the Lord will not despise. Every time you fall, get back up and start again. Proverbs 24:16 ***"For a just man falleth seven times,***

and riseth up again: but the wicked shall fall into mischief."

It is okay to start over with God. I promise you God doesn't mind starting over with you. It just means you get to be the clay while He is the potter yet another time. Embrace it and never give up on the desire to be transformed. I eventually started living the way His word instructed me to, but I didn't do it; literally, I didn't do it myself. Had I kept trying and trying, I would have been in an endless cycle of trying and never succeeding. I Fasted, prayed, and read His word and made room for Him to work on me, even when I was failing during the process. Then that moment came when it was no longer I but His Holy Spirit that changed me. Here are a few things I have learned from that experience:

- **Will Power doesn't work for long. We can only resist and try for so long with our own power, but eventually, we give in.**

- **Before you give in, the enemy minimises your consequences and makes you think it is okay to do it. Then, that failure is connected to your identity, making you think you are a spiritual failure.**

- **The key to changing is in our identity. We are not what we did; we are who God says we are.**

- **If we are in Christ, He says: we are forgiven, there is no condemnation, we are the righteousness of God, and we are overcomers.**

- **When you know who you are, you know what to do.**

- **When we recognize we belong to Jesus, it changes everything.**

- **We live out who we are in Jesus by walking in the spirit, not the flesh.**

- **Wake up and depend on the spirit. Walk with the spirit.**

- **We do not change by willpower; we change by the Spirit of God.**

It is only through the word of God and by the guidance of the holy spirit that we can be transformed. Read the word of God every day. Invite His presence in all your decision-making, do not depend on yourself to get it right; you won't get it right. Allow the holy spirit to guide you in the right direction through His word. Be obedient and practise daily discipline. Even if you fail at times, remember to start over because His grace is sufficient, His strength is made perfect in your weakness ***2 Corinthians 9:12,*** and He holds no record of your wrong-doings ***Psalm 130:3.***

When you continue to dive into God's word, you will take note of His many promises to you that will strengthen you when you are weak. To be transformed is vital to being saved. Just know we are not perfect, but we have a perfect creator and father. Know that it's only through Him that we can live and maintain a holy life that's acceptable in His sight. Always be open to receiving His abundant grace that is dispensed to us daily. BE TRANSFORMED! IT CAN HAPPEN! ALLOW IT TO HAPPEN.

QUESTION 5

What is Baptism and why do we need it?

Now that we know we ought to be baptised, and it's a step in our journey as children of God. Firstly, let us understand what it means.

In the book of ***Romans 6:3-4,*** Paul says

"Know ye not, that so many of us as were baptised into Jesus Christ were baptised into his death? Therefore we are buried with him by baptism into death: that like as Christ was raised up from the dead by the glory of the Father, even so we also should walk in newness of life."

Anytime I read this verse, I have to re-read it. It is such a profound verse. Let's first analyse what verse 3 is saying to us. It says we are baptised into Jesus' death. What does Jesus' Death symbolise? John 3:16 says, ***"For God so loved the world that he gave his only begotten son that whosoever believes in him shall not perish but have everlasting life."***

The above verse highlights the love God has towards us. He loves you and I, so, He sent His son; to do what? To die for us. Romans 5:8 says, "**But God commendeth his love towards us, in that, while we were yet sinners Christ died for us.**"

Now when you get baptised, you are in acceptance of God's love towards you. In addition, as verse 4 declares, "You are buried with Him—by baptism—into death. Let's simplify this: now when you are being baptised, and you go under the water, consider yourself dead as with Christ. You have died; the old you have died. The second phrase of the above verse says, "***that like as christ was raised up from the dead by the glory of the father, even so we also should walk in newness of life.***" Just as Christ was raised from the dead, when we are raised up out of the water during baptism, we are risen in the newness of life. Our old life doesn't exist anymore, but we have become new creatures in Christ. We have now experienced Jesus' death and resurrection in our bodies. Jesus died for our sins; we have been baptised in His death; our sins no longer belong to us; it has been eradicated by Jesus' Blood. Romans 6:6 says, ***"Knowing this, that our man is crucified with him, that the body of sin might be destroyed, that***

henceforth we should not serve sin anymore." Knowing this, we have been born in sin, but God prepared something from the beginning of time to rescue us from the stain of sin. Psalm 51:5 says, ***"Behold I was shapen in iniquity; and in sin did my mother conceive me."*** However, God says in Genesis 3:15, "***And I will put enmity between thee and the woman, and between thy seed and her seed; it shall bruise thy head, and thou shalt bruise his heel."***

God set it up perfectly to redeem His children. The above scripture was a prophecy announced and prophesied to his people more than once. Genesis 3:15 speaks of how He would ensure the defeat of sin and the father of it. Putting enmity between the serpent and the woman meant there would be hostility and conflict among them. The bruising of the head and the heel represents the enemy's success in Jesus's death but Jesus's victory through the laying down of His own life and the resurrection of His death. This prophecy subsists throughout the beginning of time in Isaiah 7:14 ***"Therefore the Lord himself shall give you a sign; behold, a virgin shall conceive, and bear a son, and shall call his name Immanuel."*** The seed of the women is Immanuel; it is Jesus Christ of Nazareth. It is He who redeemed our life from destruction and crowned us with his loving-kindness. Jesus foretold his death in **Matthew 12:40** *"For as Jonas was three days and three nights in the whale's belly; so shall the son of man be three days and three nights in the heart of the earth".* Jesus' death and resurrection are the gospel; it is the power of God unto salvation to everyone ***Romans 1:16***. Baptism symbolises our faith in this gospel and the acceptance of Jesus' love upon us. Accepting that He died for our sins and that we have the liberty to be free from the sinful nature of which we were born in—by confessing our belief in the gospel and receiving baptism for deliverance from the power of indwelling sin.

In a nutshell, Baptism symbolises newness in our life. Our old man of sinful nature is destroyed, and we become free from sin.

It is an act of both our faith and obedience. Baptism symbolises this old life being put to death.

Why do we get baptised?

1. Follow the example of Jesus Christ. ***Matthew 3:13-17***

2. Obey the commands of Jesus Christ. ***John 3:3-7***

3. To be a witness that you are a disciple of Christ. ***Acts 22:15-16***

4. To receive the promise of the Holy Spirit. ***Acts 2:37-38***

5. To become a new creature. **2 Corinthians 5:17** & ***Romans 6***

QUESTION 6

Which Religion is the correct one?

When I hear Religion, I think of "schism": Separation of the people. We were called to be one in Christ because every believer is a member of Christ's body. 1 Corinthians 12:12 states, ***"For as the body is one, and hath many members, and all the members of that body, being many, are one body so is Christ."*** Religion was created by humanity. I truly believe who we identify as our saviour and Lord is imperative in our lives. I don't believe there is a typical religion that overrules every other. However, in Acts 11:26 this is where the disciples were first called Christians. **"And when he had found him, he brought him unto Antioch. And it came to pass, that a whole year they assembled themselves with the church, and taught much people. And the disciples were called Christians first in Antioch."**

Nevertheless, our faith in the true and living God is what sets us apart. Who we worship, who we pray to and the evidence of the God we serve should be evident in our lives. I would like to share a few scriptures with you;

Psalm 115:3-8

"Not unto us, O Lord, not unto us, but unto thy name give glory, for thy mercy, and for thy truth's sake. Wherefore should the heathen say, where is now their God? But God is in the heavens: he hath done whatsoever he hath pleased. Their idols are silver and gold, the work of men's hands. They have mouths, but they speak not: eyes have they, but they see not: They have ears, but they hear not: noses have they, but they smell not: They have hands, but they handle not: feet have they, but they walk not: neither speak they through their throats. They that make them are like unto them; so is everyone that trusteth in them."

The verses above shed light on how the Lord is exalted above all idols. The so-called gods the heathens worshipped in ancient times couldn't move an inch; in fact, they had to be carried. Can you imagine worshipping a god that cannot hear you—although it has ears, but can't speak to you? Although it has a mouth, but can't talk, it has legs, but can't walk, or come to your rescue? Is that even a God? God isn't made by humans, but God made humans. The true and all-powerful God cannot be compared to anyone, not even humans; however, He can become human as He pleases. ***Philippians 2:6-7 says, "Who, being in the form of God, thought it not robbery to be equal with God: but made himself of no reputation, and took upon him the form of a servant, and was made in the likeness of men."***

This is witnessed in Matthew 1: 18-25. You can read the gospels for more intel on this.

My point here is we should never argue about whose religion is correct or better. But instead, who's the God you serve, who is your Lord and Saviour, who do you pray to, who instructs you and teaches you in the way you should go? In whom do you put your faith? ***1 Corinthians 2:5*** declares, ***"That your faith should not stand in the wisdom of men, but in the power of God."*** There must be power exuding from the God you have your faith in. Or else how did you come about having faith in something/someone that hasn't given you a reason to have faith in?

I love the story of how Elijah was contesting the prophets of Baal in

1 Kings 18:17-39. Please read it. In this story, people were opportune to witness God's power and build their faith in Elijah's God. In the end, this was the people's response; ***"And when all the people saw it, they fell on their faces: and they said, The Lord, he is the God; the Lord, he is God".*** If you desire to know the "IT" the people saw, I urge you to read 1 Kings 18—particularly, verses 18-39 of that book or google it.

QUESTION 7

If I backslide, will God accept me again?

A lot of people assume that once they have made a mistake and turned their backs on God, God will do the same to them. However, God is the antithesis of mankind. He isn't like us at all. When we find it difficult to forgive others who have done us wrong, God doesn't. Once you have learnt and studied the character of God, you will understand this better.

Do you know how many times different characters in the Bible turned their back on God; ran from Him, denied Him, and made countless mistakes? More than you can count; I say this because there were moments when a whole nation rebelled against God, and He still came to their rescue. He always did. Know that He will always come to your rescue and welcome you with open arms. Know that God loves you, and there is nothing you can do or say that will make Him love you any less.

Romans 8: **35-39** declares: ***"Who shall separate us from the love of Christ? shall tribulation, or distress, or persecution, or famine, or nakedness, or peril, or sword? As it is written, For thy sake we are***

killed all the day long; we are accounted as sheep for the slaughter. Nay, in all these things we are more than conquerors through him that loved us. For I am persuaded that neither death, nor life, nor angels, nor principalities, nor powers, nor things present, nor things to come, Nor height, nor depth, nor any other creature, shall be able to separate us from the love of God, which is in Christ Jesus our Lord."

Do you know that God loves us so much that He sent His only begotten son to die for our sins? Read ***John 3:16*** again. Imagine God sending His Son Jesus to die for us, and when we disappoint Him, He decides not to accept us again. Would you agree that His death would now be in vain as it wouldn't serve its purpose anymore? He died to save us, and now, when it's time to save us by extending grace daily, do you truly believe He would neglect and forsake us during our weakest moments when we truly need Him? Nay, he would not. In fact, Jesus is at the right hand of God, making intercession for us daily ***Romans 8:34.***

Romans 8:32 says, "***HE THAT SPARED NOT HIS OWN SON BUT DELIVERED HIM UP FOR US ALL, HOW SHALL HE NOT WITH HIM ALSO FREELY GIVE US ALL THINGS."***

I capitalised the above verse because I want you to understand that God chose you and me. He wasn't forced to love us. He willingly delivered His son for the redemption of mankind. Furthermore, God, Himself put on human flesh and came into this world as a servant, as a Son just for **you** and **I**. He decreased Himself and made Himself vulnerable for **you,** and **me.** I encourage you to meditate on this for a while:

Philippians 2:7-8

But made himself of no reputation, and took upon him the form of a servant, and was made in the likeness of men: And being found in fashion as a man, he humbled himself, and became obedient unto death, even the death of the cross.

God was only God the creator until He considered you and me and became God the Son. He split Himself into two while still remaining whole in the fullness of His power. Who says God doesn't love you? Who says God wouldn't accept you again? It doesn't matter how often you backslide; God anticipates your return. Do you know that God is married to the backsliders? ***Jeremiah 3:14*** says

Turn, O backsliding children, saith the LORD; for I am married unto you: and I will take you one of a city, and two of a family, and I will bring you to Zion:

This was the second message God sent to backslidden Judah. It didn't matter how many times they messed up; God always sent a word to remind them that He will never leave, He will always accept them again. He will not give them a bill of divorce. Know that God will not divorce you and me. He will indeed chastise us and reprimand us but will always accept and forgive us. The word declares that whom the Lord loveth, he chasteneth ***(Hebrews 12:6).*** Because He loves you, He wants to correct you, He wants you to acknowledge your mistakes and seek forgiveness. I think you are in the right place if you start to think your sin is overwhelming that you cannot go to God. This means you are being convicted of your sin, and you are aware that God doesn't dwell in a mess. It means your heart is still in its fleshy state, and you are susceptible to spiritual pruning. But I never want you to stay in a phase of total condemnation. Take heed to those convictions and reproaches, cry out if you have to, and ask God for His forgiveness and He will willingly disperse His grace upon you. ***1***

John 1:9 says, ***If we confess our sins, he is faithful and just to forgive us our sins, and to cleanse us from all unrighteousness.*** He is waiting for you to confess it to Him; He knows it already. He desires for you to acknowledge it and depend on Him for daily renewal. He knows that we all sin and fall short of His glory ***Romans 3:23;*** however, His grace is sufficient ***2 Corinthians 12:9.*** His compassion doesn't fail towards us, and His mercies are new every morning ***Lamentations 3:23***.

In the book of Luke 15, Jesus, Himself shared a few parables with the Pharisees after they murmured of His socialisation with sinners. I want to share these parables with you:

1. Firstly, He talks about a man having a hundred sheep, and if he loses one, he leaves the ninety-nine to go and search for the lost one. And once the man finds the lost sheep, he lays it on his shoulder and rejoices. That lost sheep is you; the shepherd is Jesus, and he is searching for you. Can you imagine how He will feel when He finds you with an open heart ready to be accepted by Him, yet another time? He will rejoice, and not only Him but joy will be in heaven over you

when you repent and turn back to God. ***Luke 15:4-7. I encourage you to read it for yourself.***

2. Secondly, He speaks of a woman who has ten pieces of silver; if she loses one piece, she will do everything in her power to retrieve the lost one. She will light a candle, sweep the entire house, and seek diligently for that lost silver. Just as that silver is important to that woman, so are you to God. God is diligently seeking you out, desiring His children but He will not force Himself on us. His word declares, ***"Behold I stand at the door and knock, if any man hears my voice, and open the door, I will come in to him, and will sup with him, and he with me." Revelation 3:20*** He is waiting for you to let him in meanwhile, you are wondering if He will ever accept you again. Jesus continues by saying once the woman has found her silver, she calls her friends and neighbours, asking them to rejoice with her because she has found what was lost. He ends that parable by saying, ***"Likewise, I say unto you there is joy in the presence of the Angels of God over one sinner that repenteth." Luke 15:8-10***

3. Lastly, Jesus shares the parable of the prodigal son. This is a common story for everyone; however, I

will summarise it in case you have never heard of it. This man had two sons, and the younger son insisted that his father give him his portion of the money/goods that he was to inherit. Days after he received his portion, he left home, travelled to a different country, and enjoyed his inheritance so much that he wasted it all. Unfortunately, there came a famine upon the land, and he was in need, but he didn't have anything left. He then got a job working with swines. He was famished to the point that he ate the pigs' food because no one cared or gave him anything in that country. Eventually, he came to his senses and reflected on how his father's servants were living a better life than he was. So, he planned to return home, seek his father's forgiveness, and ask to work as a servant. He thought to himself that he wasn't worthy to be called his father's son anymore. Have you ever thought you are not worthy anymore to be called a child of the living God? Good thing this parable didn't end here. Neither would it end here for you. As the son was returning home, his father noticed him from afar and immediately had compassion, ran, fell on his neck, and kissed him. Jesus is saying this is what happens when a child of God returns to His Father. He doesn't condemn him, He doesn't reject him, but He extends His love and grace towards him.

What I found fascinating was how the father gave him the finest robe, put a ring on his finger, and shoes on his feet. When you come back to God, He will clothe you with what you have been lacking while out of His presence. Furthermore, the father in the parable returned his son to his rightful position: royalty, not a servant. You are a chosen people, a royal priesthood, a peculiar people. ***1 Peter 2:9*** God chose you and will continue to choose you just as the father in the parable of the prodigal son. ***Psalms 145:8-9*** declares, ***"The Lord is gracious, and full of compassion; slow to anger and of great mercy. The Lord is good to all: and his tender mercies are over all his work."*** Thinking about the marvellous work of God: nature, animals, humans, sun, moon, stars, and the universe, God's tender mercies are said to be over all of His handy work. God's mercies will always be extended towards us; Isaiah 40:10 says, "***For the mountains shall depart, and the hills be removed; but my kindness shall not depart from thee."*** Do you know what it takes to remove a mountain or hill? It takes a lot; however, it is possible, but God says it is impossible to remove His loving kindness from us. If you thought removing a hill or mountain would be hard, try removing God's kindness from yourself or anyone else. God won't remove His kindness and grace from you, so do not attempt to remove it by rejecting Him or staying away from His presence or word. His grace remains the same, and it's stuck with you. Meditate upon these verses below, especially when you find yourself thinking as the prodigal son did.

Psalm 103:8-14

"The LORD is merciful and gracious, Slow to anger, and plenteous in mercy. He will not always chide: Neither will he keep his anger for ever. He hath not dealt with us after our sins; Nor rewarded us according to our iniquities. For as the heaven is high above the earth, So great is his mercy toward them that fear him. As far as the east is from the west, So far hath he removed our transgressions from us. Like as a father pitieth his children, So the LORD pitieth them that fear him. For he knoweth our frame; He remembereth that we are dust."

My sisters and brothers in Christ, God says yes, He will accept you again, over and over and over again. Accept His abundant grace and aim to live a life that is pleasing in His sight. Pray without ceasing, read His word, stay in His presence, worship Him, praise Him, and fellowship with those in Christ. Be edified, be encouraged, and sharpen one another's iron. Stay in love and unity.

QUESTION 8

Do I have to attend Church to go to Heaven?

A lot of people pose this question to make their decision to not attend church an easy one. They would say "If I don't go to church today will I go to hell?" No, going to hell or Heaven has nothing to do with attending church. However, God does encourage us to fellowship, be edified, grow in Him, and worship. And fulfilling what his word encourages us to do can lead us to eternal glory.

When we search the Bible we find Jesus, Himself in the temple. It started when He was a youth. At the age of twelve, Jesus, upon His own will, stayed behind in Jerusalem to be in the temple. Mary and Joseph were searching for Him and when they found Him, He was listening to the teaching and He even asked questions. This story can be found in ***Luke 2:41-52***. This is a perfect example of how we, as children of God, ought to be: willingly and passionately interested in the things of God. We should desire to be in church, to learn more about His word and even ask questions about anything our curious minds desire to know. Being in church contributes to your spiritual tenacity and growth. In verse ***52*** of the above chapter, it says, ***"and Jesus increased in wisdom and stature, and in favour with God and man."***

Now, when we give our life over to Christ; we are a novice and have become like babies before Him and His word. We lack the knowledge, understanding, wisdom, and power we ought to have walking in our new life. Yes, we have the word of God (Bible) to guide us; however; many of us do need a shepherd to teach us of the things that are now new to us. Some people get overwhelmed when they open the Bible; they do not know where to start and do not understand a lot, and there are some awesome critical thinkers—like you, who need to know the why, who, what, and where behind everything. Attending church and being under the right leadership is where you start. **1 Peter 2:2** says, "As newborn babes, desire the sincere milk of the word, that ye may grow thereby." When you desire the sincere milk of the Word, you would be interested in hearing the teachings of the Word of God. Going to Bible studies or Sunday school and services feeds that hunger for more of God's word.

However, a good shepherd would encourage you to seek and know God for yourself outside of church gatherings. Like reading, praying, worshipping, and fasting. By attending church, you will learn of the different ways in which you can build a relationship with God for yourself. It is imperative that we know God for ourselves. We must maintain personal relationships with God outside of church gatherings. There should be a balance of both. Encouraging both is the neutral thing, and it is paramount that we attend church and continue to seek God for ourselves. Some people attend church but do not have a relationship with God outside it. They never pray on their own; their Bible is only open on Sundays or Saturdays; they do not fast unless the church initiates it; they do not worship on their own. They truly do not know who God is outside of what the pastor or people have mentioned Him to be.

Do not attend church just to mark your attendance and to say you attend church but neglect your personal relationship with God.

Practising both is essential. If you have developed an unshakeable relationship with God at home, that is a major plus; however, join a church that aligns with God's truth, preaches the word, and lives by it. ***Ephesians 4:11-12*** says, ***"And he gave some, apostles; and some prophets, and some, evangelist; and some, pastors and teachers; for the perfecting of the saints, for the work of the ministry; for the edifying of the body of christ."*** God gave the above so we, as children of God, can be edified as Paul edified the churches in the Bible; some of which He was able to teach in a temple, on the streets, and even send letters from prison. Paul understood the importance of edifying the body of Christ, so he made every effort to go to them to share what God laid on his heart or put ink to paper in prison. He continues in verses 13-14 of the above chapter and book by saying, ***"Till we all come in the unity of the faith, and of the knowledge of the son of God, unto a perfect man, unto the measure of the stature of the fullness of Christ. That we henceforth be no more children, tossed to and fro, and carried about with every wind of doctrine, by the sleight of men, and cunning craftiness, whereby they lie in wait to deceive; but speaking the truth in love, may grow up unto him in all things, which is the head, even Christ."***

Paul understood that if we didn't have a solid foundation in Christ, we could be easily swayed into some other doctrine that isn't God's truth. He aimed to encourage us to be one in the body of Christ in faith and knowledge of Jesus Christ. He wants us to grow in the things of God; he desires our faith to stand in the power of God and not in the wisdom of men (***1 Corinthians 2:5***). Attending church contributes to the above. Although some people have had terrible experiences in church, I truly believe the pros outweigh the cons. Here are a few impacts attending church has on you as an individual and the body of Christ as a whole:

1. Invites the presence of God: Matthew 18:20 says, "***For where two or three are gathered together in my name, there am I in the midst of them.***"

2. Encourages and edifies one another: Colossians 3:16 says, "***Let the word of Christ dwell in you richly in all wisdom; teaching and admonishing one another in psalms and hymns and spiritual songs, singing with grace in your hearts to the Lord.***"

3. Increases your faith: Romans 10:17 says, "***So then faith cometh by hearing, and hearing by the word of God.***"

4. Delivering and receiving exhortation: Hebrews 10:24-25 says, "***And let us consider one another to provoke unto love and to good works: Not forsaking the assembling of ourselves together, as the manner of some is; but exhorting one another: and so much the more, as ye see the day approaching.***"

5. We function as a body and operate in our gifts: Romans 12:4-8 says, "***For as we have many members in one body, and all members have not the same office: So we, being many, are one body in Christ, and every one members one of another. Having then gifts differing according to the grace that is given to us, whether prophecy, let us prophesy according to the proportion of faith; Or ministry, let us wait on our ministering: or he that teacheth, on teaching; Or he that exhorteth, on exhortation: he that giveth, let him do it with simplicity; he that ruleth, with diligence; he that sheweth mercy, with cheerfulness.***"

6. Promotes a reverence for God and encourages unbelievers to become a part of God's family: Acts 9:31 says, "***Then had the churches rest throughout all Judaea and Galilee and Samaria, and were***

edified; and walking in the fear of the Lord, and in the comfort of the Holy Ghost, were multiplied."

7. Receiving of prayers and healing: James 5:17 says, "***Is any sick among you? let him call for the elders of the church; and let them pray over him, anointing him with oil in the name of the Lord:"***

I want to include that although we go to a building, the building is not the church. Everyone goes to the building to meet up with the church. We are the church. The building is a place where the church gathers. We are the church, and we are not confined to the four corners of a building.

About The Author

Frenica Williams is a teacher by profession. She is from the beautiful island of the Turks and Caicos Islands. She is a single lady who is passionate about the things of God. She is also passionate about children. She is a voracious reader; however, she was led to write this book under the inspiration of the Spirit of God. She was first lead in 2022; she started writing late that year, but there was a delay in the writing. God stirred up the desire to continue to write in 2023, and she completed this book in January 2024 with the Grace of the almighty God.

www.ingramcontent.com/pod-product-compliance
Lightning Source LLC
Chambersburg PA
CBHW070815050426
42452CB00011B/2049
* 9 7 8 1 3 9 9 9 7 7 9 3 7 *